Lucy Dougan's new collection draws on the mysterious zone that Surrealist artist Paul Nash called 'Monster Field': the place glimpsed from a car at speed, which opens up a space between the everyday and the occult as it 'almost slides past your eyes'. Like a monster, 'elusive and ubiquitous' a poem is a 'showing' of what is both unsettling and familiar. Mundane or discarded objects, fleeting scenes and inconsequential places can become unexpectedly charged with momentary significance and rise up as weird extremities in the field of the ordinary. Dougan's ongoing concerns – the hidden or unperceived, things out of place, the intrusion of wildness into ordered spaces, the shifting relationship between past and present – are deepened in this collection by the disorientations of middle age: in experiences of survival, difficulty, and failure; and in the presence and pressure of mystery.

Dougan's elliptical work hints at a life that hovers just beyond our comprehension; in dreams, tales, the past, in the imagination of the poet. This other world surrounds even the most domestic of the poems. WA Premier's Poetry Award

Also by Lucy Dougan

Memory Shell
White Clay
On the Circumvesuviana
Meanderthals
Wild Estate
The Guardians

LUCY DOUGAN

MONSTER FIELD

NEW POEMS

GIRAMONDO

First published 2022
from the Writing and Society Research Centre
at Western Sydney University
by the Giramondo Publishing Company
PO Box 752
Artarmon NSW 1570 Australia
www.giramondopublishing.com

Cover and design by Jenny Grigg
Typesetting by Andrew Davies
in 9/15 pt Tiempos Regular

Printed and bound by Ligare Book Printers
Distributed in Australia by NewSouth Books

A catalogue record for this
book is available from the
National Library of Australia.

ISBN: 978-1-922725-37-0

The Giramondo Publishing Company acknowledges the support
of Western Sydney University in the implementation of its book
publishing program.

This project has been assisted by the Commonwealth Government
through the Australia Council, its arts funding and advisory body.

WESTERN SYDNEY
UNIVERSITY
Australian Government
Australia Council for the Arts

I.M. Lesley Eva Dougan

For Max and Jonathan Dolin

Monster Field. Where, where? Over there, to the left, the next field beyond the hedge. It was always the same, elusive and ubiquitous.
Paul Nash

Contents

II

III

I

It was true that I had no idea how to endure being alive and everything that comes with it.
Deborah Levy

The Throne

In crisis
I go to the local library
and do not take out
the book I find,
this one or that one first,
what matter?
Outside beside my car
sits a strange chrome and vinyl seat,
part of a vanity set,
stranded, hieratic, ruined,
like the beautiful straight-backed
low-seated chair-people
of Saint-Martin-d'Ardèche.
I do the visual maths.
Will it fit behind?
– no, there, rightfully, is the seat for our grandson –
I consign its odd allure to my phone's photo bank instead.
I sit on it only once,
open its cream frayed seat
with its tooled insignia of promise
– *nothing* –
What does it mean
for home to be a failure?
What does it mean
for other places to be a failure?
I leave the throne to its own
mise en scène, neither

desolate nor replete
were I to claim it.
There is, after all, no mirror
in front of which to place it
though I fix my hair and do my lips
before I reverse away.

Why You Stopped Making Things

Driving, you tell me
why it is
you stopped making things.
It was the terrible pressure,
you said, the terrible pressure
you felt that everything
must have significance,
and worse, significance for you
alone. You couldn't bear it.

I keep trying to look sideways at you.
I keep trying to feel the windscreen wipers
you have activated in my eyes so that my lashes
will clear the view.
Can I tell you
that your car suits the city,
that this rain suits the city,
that your car in the rain
suits the city?
I can't tell what is now okay
to make something of
or not.

Art Detective

I lie on the couch
like a beaten dog
as Philip Mould advances
his latest art forensics
and there are these absolutely
loose and liberated daubs
of greens and browns
in close-up on the screen.
They are of the earth
in a surprising way, counter
to all that brocade, country houses,
rich people by the yard.
And from my beaten-dog pose
I fall in love with Gainsborough.
How could I have not before?

Philip Mould's suit combos are impeccable.
He is always consulting experts,
always moving crisply through the
weak light of investigation sites
– the galleries – but his eyes
look infinitely tired
as if he has done so much
looking for us.
I trust his close-ups.

After enough experts
and trailing about,
there is Gainsborough again
with his louche letters
and unsympathetic wife,
his treatment of vests
and his small garden tray arrangements
that look a lot like the moss tray
gardens of childhood
only more elaborate
with water features
and places to arrange a nymph or two
or a satyr.
They are a step up from what one
could get at the model shops,
though proximate, small feathery trees
and a brittle feeling of those bags
full of fake glittering lawn.

It leaves me unaccountably sad
that Gainsborough had to live with someone
who threw out all his dirty letters.
What a loss Philip Mould's co-host
says off her guard, passionately,
as the camera hovers over the tray garden
– this little grave of creativity.
And she's right.

Crumpled

I need to sit with myself again
to know how I felt
before I got crumpled.
There's a lithograph of feeling crumpled
by Dame Paula Rego.
The undoing is recorded
in every mark of the etching needle
as if its maker
were in such a rage, in such despair,
that she flailed at it then tore it up in tiny pieces
and then put it back together
by a magic no one can see.
It's of Jane Eyre ugly,
not Jane Eyre prettified;
and she's lying at ground zero
beneath her monstrously hatched skirts
in the room at Gateshead Hall.
And yet there's no room,
only the sheet of
miraculously restored paper
with all the crumples alive.
On TV Sheila Hancock asks Dame Paula:
Have you ever felt like that, so like that?
Oh yes, she answers in the most phlegmatic of ways.

Features on Artistic Women Who Live by the Sea in UK Magazines

They are dark-haired, solitary types
who ill-advisedly have pushed on, wearing
black spidery shawls and long full skirts.
They look as though they might, in years past,
have been done by Augustus John or Julia Margaret Cameron.
All that waiting around and holding onto wan expressions,
it's still the go.

And we must bear weary testament
to their perfect upcyclings
tastefully displayed,
those post-Bloomsbury concoctions
of textiles and bleached furniture, boxes
painted in the style of Matisse.

Any mess or mark of effort
is polished away
to the smoothness of
the pebbles in that bowl over there.
Witch's stones are the ones
with the holes
reads the caption.
Maybe it gets terribly cold
and pretty lonely
in Suffolk or in Devon
with or without the perfect children
who are tidied away

beyond their playroom and the lens.
Perhaps they are truanting at the offy
(the lives of bohemians' children
are rarely swell).
And maybe it gets tougher
finding the 'finds'
that will delight the sub-editor's eye,
trawling the edges for such low pay.

Artistic women who live by the sea,
I've changed my mind.
I hope that patrons come in droves to your doors
and pay mightily for what you make.
I hope that the wind comes as friend,
as divine inspiration, not as foe,
and that you stand always
just outside this peddling of your art.
Let it be for sale, but not imprisoned
in these creamy, heavy pages
with the spreads
for pricey anti-ageing creams
knocking just next door.

The Dolls

They are shut up in a box
yet the privation they endure
was never my intention.
Once they sat in the centre of things
with the loud silence
that dolls can own.
But they frightened the children.
The smallest would tiptoe past
with eyes closed.

An old handmade doll
is a strange makeshift business,
an agreement between
any number of materials
to come together,
to stay together.
Is this what scared the children?
Is this what drew me to them –
their little tilt
of what it is
to be feminine, human?

I still remember the texture
of the day I found the dolls.
I swung down the street
feeling open, reckless,
and I swear the dolls called to me

from deep in a display case
in the second-hand shop.
I paid for their unknown provenance,
the standing one, the seated one,
both very old.

To this day, I think of it
as a return –
the moment I bought myself back –
agreed that warring selves
could live beneath my skin.
No wonder the dolls frightened everyone
and could only later be borne
in tiny glimpses.

Home Economics

Ecco hommo, as we joked about it,
was clearly about being tied up
in knots of time wasting; about humiliation,
performance. What the fuck
is the golden triangle
of a kitchen anyway?
I thought it was somewhere unlocatable
in *Ripley's Believe It Or No*t from 1978.
Or wait. That's the one in Bermuda.
This would be a good place
(Latitude: 25° 00' 0.00" N
Longitude: –71° 00' 0.00" W)
to disappear all time and motion tortures
before you go missing yourself.
And also activity sheets
involving being tethered
to yet another kind of string
in which you had to draw the snare line
to match shoes to an outfit.
Go ahead.
Put the vampish mules
with the work overalls
and the high-tops with the wedding dress
and run, run for your life, and forget
how Debrett's teaches a lady to alight from a car.
Flash your triangle all you like.

Highschool Sewing

Wincey – but
really – wincey,
a baby word
from a nursery rhyme
is what was doled out
by the metre.

You could make a layette, girls
because who would know
when you might need it?
Strange shapes and sizes,
dolly small or too big
for some prodigiously headed
imagined baby who would divide
heaven from earth. The thought
that you might really pop one out
was perhaps too horrific to transfer
to tracing paper.

Portion control is what it was.
Getting ready to get ripped off
in all sorts of ways.
It was practiced in Home Ec. too.
Measly sizes from magazine recipes:
toad-in-the-hole and egg-in-the-nest.
Only once when the history teacher
invaded the kitchen

did we get the taste of something else.
Don't peel the carrots leave the skins on
they're good for you.
He was curly haired and gap-toothed
with the bones of a child.

The one girl in the class
who made real things
had hands that ran
uncontrollably with sweat
and when some other girl
got extolled for her work
(*exquisite, just exquisite*)
we lost it together
behind the poke-hole frames of our machines
Husqvarnas on one side and *Berninas* on the other –
all the man-made borders of that class
– we were banished from Switzerland/Sweden
to the barren quadrangle
where we were sat still on opposite sides
holding flat bellies,
the laughter pains in them
sharp little heralds
of what we might birth later
and clothe in anything
but wincey.

The Monkey Face Bag

I buy the bag with the monkey face
from the girl with the faltering hands
and the slow, deliberate voice.
We agree it's a good price.
It just came in today.
The monkey has a large mouth
as if he had opened it wide
and found nothing to say.
She tells me that she likes the monkey brand.
It's a gift for my niece
I explain as I pay.
It's one for surfies. Does she surf?
I picture my niece, her neat shape,
hovering above us on a wave.
I shake my head hesitantly,
driving other customers away.
I think our chat is done
then she tells me
once she had pyjamas
with the monkey face
that were too tight.
As she struggles with the change
I ask the price of a wooden ornament
until she gets it right.

The bag with the monkey face
swallows the day.

I ride the swell of a headache,
swap texts with my sister.
We are both okay.
My niece used to like the monkey brand
but my sister is not sure now.
So I put it high in the cupboard
with other things that do not fit.
Stretching up into the dark
I find the girl from the shop
freed from her endless transactions,
curled asleep beneath a sea of monkeys;
each surprised mouth
stretched out of sameness
by her difference.

Space Walk

I need to go back
and start with the photo,
no, the armchairs in the photo
and the people sitting in them.
I can still smell the chairs' oiled frames
and feel the not unpleasant roughness
of their slubbed fabric covers.
My father with his Gatsby looks
and clothes that sat on him
just the way they had from boyhood,
and my mother with her contained
sleek joy and her bare legs crossed
that might at any moment
curl under her contentedly.

The sleep-out is not its origin
yet I transpose the shot there,
the long low room
that wrapped around
the back of the house.

My sister lived a long time in this room
as a sculpted head
with a bun pulled back tight.
She smelt dusty. She smelt busy,
never free from her exercises
at the barre.

This is the room in which
I learned of the moon landing,
the room in which the actors came
to ask the dog, impudently, why she was sad,
and the room in which I told my family
I loved them and pillaged their books,
served out in shadow play
their ping-pong games
to my own advantage
when they were barely there.

Always from this vantage
the steps sweeping out
down to the garden, always the roses
blooming, falling.
I need to go back.

How can I run through this still thing,
the photo of the figures in the chairs,
and disturb its dense patina
of all the rooms in which it has hung
right back to the moment of its composition?

Here is the sunlit corner
partitioned by a bookcase,
where my grandmother slept
with the radio on;
one small step
densely here alive then gone.

Pansy Face

My mother has her pansy face on.
Her neck is a little wilted.
It is her version of the face
that says no admittance.
It is beautifully closed to the world.
For years I have needed her
to tell me how women survive
but I cannot expect an answer on that now.
When she does talk covertly about survival
she will say things like
remember the soldiers in the family,
remember them.
Or she will evoke the Roman stoics.
She will say
you have to think like a Roman,
you have to die like a Roman.

When my mother's face goes pansy-eyed
and her mortal colours glow,
I go to the relic of her movie scrapbook
where a chorus girl army of flower faces
stare out from her cut-outs and glue.
Even there she hasn't left me any clues.

The Narrows

One (1984)

When we took out the boat
we stood back to back.
He at the helm,
me aft,
father and child
in a well-rehearsed balance.
From side to side,
the buoy lights pulsed,
red/green, red/green,
warned us off sandbars,
showed us the deepest course.
Still bodies aboard
and flashing signals afloat,
altogether we made
a makeshift compass.
At the waist of the river
– The Narrows –
as we passed beneath the bridge
sounds bounced around
the cold shadowed columns.
For seconds, an obliteration of sky,
a sudden transportation into
a place where senses deaden
or heighten.

Two (1942)

Earlier, you sisters had your skiffs
and your freedom.
It hadn't mattered that the bridge
was not yet built.
You could find your way across
somehow or another.
Sometimes you were mortified
to have to pick up the old professors
who'd hail you down in your father's car
(these were the war years)
and who were, after all, just trying
to get round the river too.
He worked at the cinema then, your father,
and caught the ferry home.
His black cat, Robert,
waited for him at the top of the hill.
But even the wilder of you girls,
who did not model herself on the nice
ones in your movie scrapbook,
would not have been game enough
after dark to take the skiff across
at the closest part
where the water gathered
glamorous as a waist in satin.
Instead, with nothing to hold,
your sister called across that reach,
with all the ardour of a silent screen siren,
her beaux oddly relieved

that the wind and water
hurled back her voice, her terrible need,
into wavelets of script
they couldn't read.

Three (2019)

Their names called out again,
and again, loudly in a perfect round
so that the sound jolts us from our sleep
but does not wake you.
Your first companions,
your sister, your cousin
who is later your husband.
Your sister, your cousin,
small children in an immensity of fields,
or by the sea, guarded by solid folk
but still always an inviolate three:
you, your sister, your cousin/husband.
In the next room
the otherworldliness of your task
tethers us to our bed.
In rounds again and louder again,
your sister, your cousin,
as if you summon them
across a widening strait,
or has your sleep-talk
brought them close?
If we were brave enough
we'd submit to this maelstrom,

lash ourselves
beneath the bridge
where your voice
bounces off the dead
and subsides as suddenly
as it started.

The Creatures That You Lived With in Your End Days

One or so had names.
Ben the blue-tongue,
I remember him
and some of his dietary preferences.
Milk was it?
The others like the daddy-long-legs
in the bathroom were nameless
yet still loved.
You lived with them lightly,
uncomplicatedly, until the night
you thought you were dying.
You had the Sonnets there with you.
You had dog-eared pages one apiece
for the three of us
to match our tempers, how you saw us.
I know you thought
each little song a planet
and you were right about that
but not about your own end
which was close but later.
We washed your clothes.
Took your challenge of a dog
back to the city.
And that was that.

Blue-Black

These days
I'm fading.
I have to colour myself in,
lips, brows, lashes, hair,
with little tools
that I've never really understood.
I thank fate for my mother,
so oblivious to all of this,
and for my daughter,
great confident wielder of kohl.
And I am somewhere in between,
flat on the slab at the beautician's.
With eyes bandaged shut against cold dye,
blue-black mothy thoughts press in
until the back of my mind
floods with a whole delta
of decorations applied in private,
on display. Beyond me
in the waiting room
my elegant elders
sift patiently through *National Geographic*s or *Cleo*s,
every one of their hard-earned patrician rings glinting.

Bad Painting

In the painting
she doesn't look like herself at all.
She looks like a smear
of lip gloss mixed with sand
or a half-chewed lolly on the floor.
And seeing as
lip gloss mixed with sand
and a half-chewed lolly
are sad to contemplate,
she also looks sad.

It's hard to know why the painter
would have chosen to diminish her so.
Why the colours look like
faded sherbet or those tones
of industrial foam
you see somewhere
you would not choose to walk,
by night or day.

Around the edges
she is gathering herself
though not so you could see.
Squint or walk by quickly half looking
and she changes tricks
like a holographic martyr
you'd like to take home
and fix a stiff drink for.

Your Shade

I.M. Fay Zwicky

They don't make the lipstick
you wear any more.
The small grief of this niggles you
as if some part of your armoury
or what it is that helped you face
the day is gone forever.
You enlist me in the hunt.
In the past I've done your footnotes,
faxed handwritten pages,
but this, this archive
of lost shades, is a tipping point
into something that lies
stubbornly beneath everything.

Discontinuities begin to haunt me,
the trails of product codes
guttering out to deadstock.
I get close but then
it all packages itself
into a terrible grasping
faux proximity, a smear, a ghost
print on a tissue
hidden in the cuff
of your cardigan.
And I never ask you
the million-dollar question:

how does it feel
to outlive a colour
that you loved?

While the decision was being made,
as the phase-out happened,
so slowly that you didn't notice,
you kept up your enquiries
at the make-up counter,
your bare lips kept moving
but the sounds they made,
the questions they asked,
began to get lost in the queue.

II

I propose a conspiracy of orphans.

John Berger

Leonie

Paid artists' model,
your face has lived with the family for decades.
You have suffered endless room changes,
the tectonic jolts of whole-house moves
yet you remain sanguine.
Your hairstyle has weathered the years
and the many rows and unkind words you have presided over,
also good times, rafts of regrettable TV.
If I were rendered blind I would know
your lightly pitted cheekbones,
your brow line, your rough underside and slight headache-inducing
scent of epoxy resin in which a finger could snag a glassy splinter
of what it is you keep inside the void of your cast.
I cannot see you as empty for in your hollow head lives the clamour
of us all.
And something else, you still abide with us
even though our mother and father are dead and gone.
Stranger, stay with us,
watch over us,
never leave us.

Extras

The eye of our sister's phone
is upon us
so at first we freeze,
arranging ourselves
for a future she tries to capture.

When we realise it's home movies
we loosen fixed smiles
and our cheeks go lax
as we pretend to chat
like extras on a set
of fake peonies, fake roses.
We hang on each other,
hang between times.

Oh no no no not yet.
I think of the Fayum portraits,
funereally alive.
To whom will our own high-coloured
dumb show look back?
Their dark eyes
so mild and kind and unconcerned
– the Fayums –
their blank quizzical regard of death
now holds static, certain
against our endless tags

in space and time
as we like and love
everything that passes.

After a Moment on Film

(Arnaud Desplechin's *Un Conte de Noël*)

Everything comes up to hit you,
is contained in that second
of lingering by the photo.
The photo is silent, of course
– and land-locked –
but the wave sound is in it,
or some whoosh of time's backwash
as disorienting as being dumped in the rough,
and with a colour, or colours,
of a day lost by water.

All the characters can say for sure
is that she was a bad driver,
is that perhaps on that day
she wasn't careful;
and that she is missed,
gone missing,
all these years set by
with the bric-a-brac on the sideboard.

Movies on the Radio

(Luca Guadagnino's *I Am Love*)

A breath in – and then
the moment when the young director
admits that making his films
will depend on a particular city
and not just any old mercantile city
but Milan, he says, is what he needs;
one floor of an anonymous palazzo,
with its drab façade
and baroque surprise of an interior
that will emit a certain light,
a certain stillness.
When that is found
so far away
from his childhood in the South,
he will hole up there with books
waiting for winter's sharpness,
for blank skies and snow
and for his eyes to rest on the shapes
of everything covered.
Working this way
he finds a necessary distance.
Working this way
in each frame his characters
are freed from his judgement.

Scenes From a Novel

after Margaret Drabble

I like the way the characters
are moved around the room.
It is not awkward,
which reviewers warn against,
but happens simply, unshowily,
so that it almost slides past your eyes.
Ash in an Aga is tamped down.
Children sleeping on the floor
are stepped over, catalogued.
It is noted that soon they won't be children.
A sister goes out to smell the night air
and her brother is about to drink
one too many drinks again.
They share the hedgehog's clumsy milk raid.
The brother thinks the creature
stupid, the sister is softer, moved
by this benign visitation.

Girl on a Rug With a Cat

Everything is connected in life. The point is to know it and to understand it.
Gillian Wearing

The girl on a rug with a cat
is an entirely decorative proposition.
She curls, the cat curls, even the rug
displays some notion of this movement
with its diverting arabesques.
Life, too, is making a start inside the girl
although she cannot know this right now.
Some contract with another is being made
even as we speak on the rug with the cat beside her.
The striped ginger cat grows its hairs.
It is not the cleverest cat.
Somewhere sometime a worker,
who cannot be revealed in this schema
but who nonetheless has left their signature
in all the curlicues, made the rug.
They weren't paid well.
Perhaps they got by.
Were they a girl with life beginning inside them?
And did they own a cat,
perhaps a goat or duck, or a pig?
In this scene a lot remains unknown,
just as it always does.

A Lakeland Wardrobe

(happy or sad depending on the year you open it)

D. Wordsworth was always peeling off wet layers.
She liked other people's clothes.
She wasn't fussy:
W. Wordsworth's coats or
Sara Coleridge's dresses
so long as they were dry.
There's a bit about a landlady at an inn
getting angry with her for turning up bedraggled.
I don't think D. Wordsworth cared one hoot.

W. Wordsworth was, believe it or not,
more dandified and went in for
embroidered waistcoats.
The waistcoats probably put some financial pressure
on those dining it up at Alfoxden.
I need to find out more
about how D. Wordsworth kept W. Wordsworth's
wardrobe sorted out for him.
I imagine a lot of mending and repurposing.

Yet when W. Wordsworth got wed
I don't think there was coat sharing any more.
There was no out-in-all-weathers for D. Wordsworth
who was heartbroken and got stuck into the laudanum.
There was no mending of any kind after that,
only the drear upstairs.

And everyone still loved D. Wordsworth and tried their best for her.
I hope at the window there was at least a caring hoot
from the wild because that is what she was herself.

The Horses I Threw Out

I wish now I had kept them,
the lustreware horses
in the red raffia bag
that I threw out in a fit of anger.
What had their wider world been
before this unhappy fate?
An unlocatable 'Planet Lustre':
their hooves cavorting on the carpet
at my mother's lover's house.
They were clearly a pastime for me
before solid memory kicked in.
Ever on after in my life
I replaced them with other miniatures
by which I felt strangely burdened
though these new herds were never close
to the kitsch plumed pluckiness of their forebears,
who had once, I think, pulled a carriage.

In the past my hands hurt them.
There were chipped and missing ears, hooves.
In our brief moment of reunion
their contours hurt me back.
O little abandoned horses,
I am sorry, I am sorry.
Where was it that we travelled,
my unharnessed companions?
I stood for a moment and felt how you were

part of something separate and together,
something gleaming, something damaged.
I stroked and stroked your jaunty angles
through a seam of the red raffia bag
collapsing inwards
on the weight of its clasp.

Knots

For Jo and Claire

My hair is longer again now.
When I lie in bed
I bunch its tangles in two
behind my head
to remember early days
when I did not re-enter the house
until the lights went up;
and when my mother chased me
once around the garden
to deal with the rank knots
that lived beneath the duplicitous
silken river running over the top.
The Mason Pearson brush was my enemy
like the calamine lotion or liberty belts
that were kept in the high blue cupboards
where I had my own imagined store
of unboxed, un-bottled goods,
my own ideas of wood
or mud or moss provisions.
That brush was also my weapon.
I hurled it down the hallway
and it landed with a satisfying whump
in the middle of my sister's bare back.
I have no memory
of what that stoush was about;
only that in my unisex clothes and bare feet
I had warred so long

until I surrendered.
It was Mary Quant's stick-on stars
that did it – o frail me, o poor simulacrum –
new bright constellations whirled around
on my cheekbones and dizzied at my temples,
and I forgot to wait outside
until the lights went up indoors.

Lindsay Street Bathroom

I bought the house for the sole purpose
of seeing the moon at a certain angle
through the high bathroom window
and because there were peace lilies in planters above the bath
and because the bath was duck-egg blue.

In that bathroom I brushed my son's teeth
(1 & 2 & 3 & 4 & 5)
moving around the way his mouth was made.
Later we sent him to a school where
teeth were an obsession.

The impulse-buy dog slept in that room at night.
When I visited her there she looked at me balefully
and I realised she was a woman like me,
a woman-dog with lousy days and ecstatic days
and bored days.

In that room, too, I did a little private dance.
It was to do with the moon, the plants, the
duck-egg blue bath, my son's teeth, the dog.

Once a guest announced
that this room was breathing.
Everyone laughed, but my laugh was an uneasy one
because it came from the dog-woman,
who was not having a good day.

My secret dance also heard that laugh.
She slid down the wall,
sat next to the absent dog,
wrapped her arms round her legs,
lay down her head and closed her eyes
in dismay.

Sudbury's Wilds

I am so childish that I could make a Kite, catch Gold Finches or build Little Ships
Thomas Gainsborough

Always in your work a sense
of the ground at your feet,
a sense of movement over
deeper coursing movement.
First forays were for flowers
your mother painted.
You must have known all the trodden ways,
added to their sum total,
and what the seasons made
when and where.
You must have known
the strange light and striations
in pale stems just grasped from the ground,
how to balance colour in your pickings.
Although eventually your keep
would come from bodies, faces,
lengths of cloth, devoted dogs,
it was your *landskips* that you loved.
You abandoned school for them,
for the feeling of being in and with
the telluric pull of Sudbury's wilds.
This is what shadows in and around
all the figures that you painted.
They are of the human world and yet
they emerge from the dark as bright roots.

Their lace is bark or lichen, their satins lie like stray ponds
and blush on their cheeks is pollen falling,
always falling as you run home.

The Claphams

for Elizabeth Smither

Lord and Lady Clapham are tired, and
let's face it, enwreathed in a genteel decrepitude.
They've lodged in the small houses
with the people so long now.
Little people are the ones that caused the
most perturbation even though Lord and Lady C.
did over all the decades
intuit something of the frenzied love a child can bestow.
This love lost them eyes, noses, fingers...*ahhhh*...*lack-a-day*.
The tall serious people in the bigger houses with the glasses and gloves,
not nearly so decorously kitted out as L & L,
fixed the eyes, the noses, the fingers –
fluffed the petticoat (the lady), relined the frock coat (the lord) –
but slowly, ever so slowly (aeons of slowness apparently)
Lord and Lady Clapham learned
that those hands, no matter how kind,
were not possessed with the same love
as the small hands in the houses with their gardens,
dangerous ponds, and pet tortoises.
In the bigger houses strangers come to gawp
at L & L. Often they do not take off their coats. Often they do not
really see through the glass.
The Claphams divinely restored – on show –
are starting to detest
the phrase 'two-for-one Sunday'.
If they could they would embrace.

The Wallpaper

The wallpaper was a forest.
You had put it up with your father.
You let me into the new dappled world
behind your desk.
When you sat in front of it
you looked like something from a painting.
After a silence
you don't like it
is all you said,
a statement,
not a question.
A simple statement
just like the paper forest
or that you loved your father
or that to your father
you were a boy in need of a forest.
It is so long ago now.
So long since you lived there.
So long since we were close
(as if we had both vanished into the well-laid depths
of the wallpaper wood with no search party sent).
And I wish,
as much as one might wish,
lost in the woods,
that I had slain
the ogre inside my skin
that did not say

your forest is beautiful,
but most of all
that it was naff
in a good way.
I was such a stupid girl
and yet there you sat
in your wood
with never a reprimand.
Down the bombed out years
I imagine you sitting there still.

Strange Plant

It was the plant that made the room strange.
No one had grown it or willed it to grow
but there it was
pushing in between the wall and the ceiling.
We all held hands around the table
in avowal of our gathering
though in retrospect it seems
that this gesture
was entirely about the plant.
Was it malicious? Or had it
provenance from somewhere: a tale,
a previous inhabitant's carelessness, a ghost?
Years back my sister had seen
what she called 'the aura'.
I connect this to broken blue glass
and a villa hemmed in
by the asphalt of an untidy car park
and not to the tiny elevated patio
and not to our hands held all together in the night.
Proprio qui, proprio ora, someone had said.
You could will yourself
not to look out of the corner of your eye,
not to see the plant pushing
into the illuminated empty room
in the first floor across the street.
You could steel yourself into believing
right here, right now
but this was in no way easy.

***Aspete*/Wait**

after Shirley Hazzard

In the *vicoli*
the great heft of washing
flaps above me,
driven by winds
that might have ancient names
or simply be *cattivi*,
sucked out and back
as if the streets themselves
are breathing.
Somewhere in the
closed chapel of Sansevero
lies the veiled Christ
in his wrappings,
miraculously light
as this bleached and hoisted lot,
the afterbirth of his crown of thorns
discarded by his side.
A short walk on
bolts and swathes of cloth
overwhelm the narrow passages.
Later in a darkened shop,
a *lavanderia*,
the patient expat helps me explain
exactly the powder that I need.
Aspete, signora, this one, right?
Aspete in his Neapolitan
becomes asssh – pet,

a meaning so close
to the remnant clouds
that have hung above this town.
Paying, I make a poor answer.
What did I wait for here
but the fine white
of not knowing
falling all over me?

Everyone Fell in Love With Duke

for Tracy and Valerie

He just wants to feel his
feet on the grass.
I gaze out longingly
to the prone figure
and the geese beyond.
The tasting is a sprawl too.
Duke's list is comprehensive, a long vertical life.
We fall into other parts of his place
(*but these glasses are beautiful*)
to find Hilde
who in her pencil sketch when young
looks fetchingly like Britt Ekland.
And I give in to the grass,
finding my predecessor's footholds,
rubbing my feet on the earth like carpet
as one of us has always done for consolation.
I think of the spaciousness
of the wedding scene in *Melancolia*.
The bride abandons the photo
of the apple orchard.
How could she?
How could she not?
And the children wander around
bored witless but happy
that they finally have an entrée into
unreadable adult ennui
for once (in sips, little stolen sips).

Friends said *don't see this film*
because a character admits
the world tastes like ash
in my mouth.
I am not ready
when one of my sons
announces the same
and yet
best not to look away.
I leave the grass for the lake,
happy to seduce the geese
but they all take flight
as I approach them quite innocently with nothing.
I want to ask the affable wine-maker
if his mellow red Morrissey
is actually named after Morrissey
(*ask me ask me ask me*)
Fat chance my husband says.
Morrissey, red?
Driving away
we decide unanimously
that we all fell in love with Duke:
his patter, his braces, his endearments,
his slipshod generous pours.
So much so that one of our companions
announces, as we navigate
the restless curves of 'the sleeping lady',
that he is quite merry.

Gillian's Prize Horse

I like the horse in that TV show
and the tension around him.
He is prized and yet he is always in his stall.
Different characters go to him at different times
to offer fealty or to tell him their woes.
When they slump down in dejection
on the cold stable floor
he can just about reach his pedigreed neck
down to comfort them.
Stay in that moment a little, his loamy breathy
horse-smell somewhere between shit and hay.
Everything is so damned terrible
for the families in that show.
I'm going to say it:
why not jump on his glossy back
and ride the hell out of it all?
Could one or two of you, at least, try to do this please?

Numbers, Sex, Gifts
(notes on strange presents that Mum bought)

Magazines that were too grown up,
American hair conditioner
(Pantene…it was exotic back then)
and navy blue crocheted singlets.
I suspect these were all from the variety supermarket
in her lover's neighbourhood
which probably no longer exists.

At the time of these gifts
I asked Mum if you could have sex
with your clothes on standing up
and she said 'of course'.
We were in the alleyway
between the classroom windows and the oval,
a sunken space,
below-ground in feeling.
Whenever I think about that conversation
I see the fully clad lovers against the alley wall.
I like those lovers. I've left them there for years
getting on politely with their congress,
oblivious to the school bell.

The 'could you have sex fully clothed standing up' question
coincided with the moment at which I began to understand
numbers in groups of ten and, curiously, this was connected
to a series of low terraced walls by the oval
beneath the pines. I had enough in my legs

to run every section of the wall in tens. I did it
again and again. Then, numbers seemed to me a beautiful arcana
that I could just grasp, that I could just fit into my stride
on walks so familiar my mind blanked.

In winter I descend the Underground
on those old solid wooden escalators.
Inside me rides the child
who stepped the low ascending walls
and kept the clothed lovers
locked tightly for so long.
We are all still travelling together
up and down – my mother too.
Everyone smells of some new piney scent
that makes me swoon before I can work out
which changes and stops I'll make;
how my legs will count them,
how my body will hold up.
Along with the child, my mother, and the lovers,
I carry the too-old-for-me magazine
that is now too young. 'Never!' she says,
in the same way she said 'of course'.

III

All the blood facts that follow me to bed at night.

Don DeLillo

The Brazier

There was something in it, then, after all,
living like this,
driving and knitting,
and waking to biscuits and milk like a child;
reduced to standing in supermarket aisles
and reading the ingredients compulsively,
admiring all the packages
too much as she had.
Her father said it was a syndrome,
this love of packaging,
and she admitted tiredly
that all those years ago
he might have been, no, was,
completely right.
She didn't have it as bad as some
or it was not such a grand scheme,
but still she had it,
a form of homelessness
that she would end up
articulating or not.
Or she would just knit and drive and dip biscuits in milk
and read the packages from which the crumbs had come.
Night was best – the outdoor night,
sitting by the brazier
that had been an afterthought anniversary present.
The bougainvillea arched above, ghostly, most alive.
Were its flowers also leaves of a different colour?

They stood out in the blackness
as if husks of burnt paper had risen – unwritten scraps,
yet still substantial,
floating, not giving anything away.

Lover Lover

When I can't see him
I think about my lover sleeping.
Once I thought I saw him
stretched out on the grass
by the river with his jumper
hiding his face.
I could tell by the undersides
of his arm flung up and his fingers
yet it could not have been him
because he was walking right next to me.
Walking next to me I forget I see him
and conclude it is possible he is outside everywhere.
For years he has been an inside proposition.
There is something about the way his hips
are a little large between my legs
and that when we kiss his lips and teeth
do not quite fit mine.
I love these sharp mismatches,
and these bodies that could or should be him
lying all over the place.

Gomi Office

The *gomi* office
sits squarely in the park
true to its materials:
a table, a chair, a phone.
It has set up shop
as they say
but the boys who made it
from the council throw-out
are not ready
for bank statements
or the solemnity
of collars and cuffs.
They have abandoned
their assemblage for other larks
so the *gomi* office bides its time
working nature.
Children slide by
the desk lamp's peripheral vision
the phone cord's reach.
At night it is perfectly at home
beneath a sliver of moon
and the trees with their leaf outlines
neat as paper cuts.
I dream a man comes to work
at the *gomi* office –
a 'one man for the use of'

kind of man,
but I cannot for the life of me
fathom the clock he will punch.

Climbing

I dreamt of him
dead now these thirty years.
Entering his world
a saturation of blue:
our clothes, the walls, the dusk,
his eyes; though he was not
as I had known him. Still young
but with a greater density of being.
I was older, older even than now.

His lap was a wrecked childhood
climbing frame, a honeycomb structure.
However I tried to settle on him
he was not stable in any way
that I could understand.
He told me that I smelt as I had always done
like I had earth in my pockets.
I told him that he reminded me
of a picture-book garden,
its overlaid pages
smutty with glitter.
When I asked him how death-time felt
he pointed out the window.
Like this, just like the sky.

On waking I felt consoled
then slept again to find him

moved on, away.
Stealthily he took his jacket from the hall
and closed the latch on the gate.
From those last acts I gauged
that he was almost certainly alive
in some other place;
that all along he had another life
and that he'd lied.

Your Bed

The young men,
friends of our middle boy,
camp nights in your bed.
Some leave it tight with hospital corners,
some like a lair they plan to come back to,
some make cocoons on top.
In most cases
they're shaping up.
Caught on kitchen raids
they all report sound sleep
and I wonder what it is
that breaches their dreams
as they lie
in this last contracted room of yours?
Can they imagine your life?
Is it this nest of photos, letters, legend –
all that dense action –
that guards their rest?
I wish for an instant
they could see as I do
the stout baby with black curls,
the girl smiling with her shoulders hunched
at the Southern Ocean,
the young doctor tending
someone in an iron lung;
and sometimes our mother
in the garden,

white glints in the air,
flowers that have floated off your dress.
And now abrupt Trojan old age.
They don't see it.
They can't.
But part of this is what keeps them
coming back, I think,
that and the allure of your
strange come-and-go arrangements.
At fifty-six
I'm thankful
for every second
you have been away
and shown us all
that there is still life
to be lived
beyond convention.

Where You Go to Sleep

When you can't sleep
you make a cave
in which you camp.
It's only completely yours
and could be inside your mind
or under the covers.
I'd ask for a map.
I'd ask for entrance.
But I know,
like a deep slumber,
it is not easily breached.

A certain perfumier
could divine ancient caves
from surrounding air alone.
Trailing banks and banks of dense fern,
he'd stop and hit the spot
at which solidity gives way
to a hidden empty fullness.

I might wish for this kind of nose,
this second sense for hollows,
but your cave would remain
untraceably yours.
Space, perhaps, for a dog, a fireplace.

Monster Field

(Royal Perth Hospital)

Can the view from a building still contain
a skyline that is lost?
I think it can.

Now I'm back for bloods.
The nurse is sweet.
He kneels to work
on a vein in the slope of my hand
with no luck
even though I belly breathe,
even though I try to imagine
a red river cascading
or platelets madly multiplying in time lapse,
screens filled with blood.
At last, it comes, here it comes!
I sense it as sound first,
life fizzing
as the vials fill.

I sense, too, my mother's and my father's
working steps within
this beating maze;
and also my younger self
swept along the corridors with the researchers strung out
after hours and finally bound for home,
their make-up smudged,
lab coats askew.

I loved it that they didn't care.
The tip-off for the secret pool,
the tunnels underground,
parties on the roof.
It was its own world, RPH,
a big ship full of shifting light,
And I was green, so green,
a bird trapped in the building
eavesdropping on all the Italian orderlies
who came and stayed and smoked
and sketched the outlines
of their villages in wavering air.

This is finally where I find my mother felled.
Her hot hand grasps mine
and she points up to the curtains
about her bed,
that colour, eau de Nil,
is what it was called,
as if this rather dingy tent
brought back to her whole swathes
of dresses made from filmy netting
and platter after platter of rabbit
passed off for chicken in the war.

I can see her handing that around,
can feel the wild brush of her foaming skirts,
green like the blur from a car window at speed.
She was so abundant, so alive inside
that tent, that old colour, then and now.

Down to the Corner

I don’t know why your death
drove me down to the corner of the house.
It was the only tolerable place to sleep.
Outside, the drains were close,
and the neighbour’s dogs,
and sometimes sounds of a child wound up.
The walls were green and chipped,
‘bok choy’, the colour we had loved
when we were young.
Your sewing box disgorged itself
on the bedside table.
The cups, the books, the recharge chords
all mounted up.
I wanted to be far away
and never out of touch.
I missed sleeping with someone.
I missed you.
I fretted at the folds of the pillowcases.
I didn’t want to touch the open end.
I didn’t want to touch the closed end.

Old Cat and Dog

The old cat and dog
now sleep in our room
in an uneasy truce
between the floor and the bed.
It's as if they are not sure
the house exists
once we no longer light it
or move about in it,
once we lie down
in agreement that it is night.
It's come to sit on my chest,
their Stilnox camaraderie,
and when I wake in snatches
I have thought different things.
Perhaps we are at sea
and this is our cabin
or perhaps without quite knowing
how or why
the rest of the house is demolished,
its surfaces wrecked, its innards divulged
in spumes of darkness.
Mornings are a strange venture.
As I keep night for them,
so they – treading out first –
herald in the day for me.

The Queue

The pilots have raindrops
beading their shoulders.
I trust these marks more than any
wings and stars.
It is as if they are half-
human half-bird waterproof creatures
with knowledge of the entire sky,
and all its weathers.

They look tired
lined up for their coffees
or whatever it is they sip.
I guess even a pilot
sleeps at night.
I think of them as the swans
we once saw at Lightcliffe;
the elegant lengths of their necks
draped artfully about their bodies,
cruising at the altitude of sleep.

King’s Cross St Pancras

Turbulent in the darkened cabin,
it’s hard to tell air from sea.
To steady myself
I recall the guide dogs
travelling the Underground.
They got to me
like nothing else on the trip.
Later, when we lay together
the first night home
I tell my husband
that I love these dogs.
At the edge of sleep
he makes his reciprocal sound.
I know this sound,
would know it anywhere,
because he made it
when each of the children was born.
Yes, he says, *the nearest station*
to the Institute for the Blind,
King’s Cross St Pancras.
The words in the name
summon the dogs again
and there they are
sitting at the feet
of unfamiliar people,
their spines
articulating freely

each jolting bend.
So much trust, I almost say,
but the one I lie with is already there,
breathing in another underground.

The Babies and Cromwell

I live at Wolf Hall for so long
that in my dream I go about with two babies.
They are good babies,
a bit of an armful, but good.
One calls Cromwell *Cremuel*
and the other calls him, *he Cromwell, Crumb*.
And one baby tells me confidingly,
the one I cradle on my left,
Cremuel crushed a snail.

My charges are getting heavy.
I'm looking for a step on which to retire
there by the river lapping – some sun
and some shade. Admirable baby
that spoke about the snail, I think
it has understood the books well.

I want to tell the babies
about the parts I like best.
Anne B. more alive in death than life
with her blue-veined feet
and her cold unwanted marmoset,
wistful for Crumb's small warm rooms,
saying she might move in one day,
saying she might well stay.
But we are all lulled on the step by the river
and fall instead into a waking silence.

Tiny Giant

(at twenty-nine weeks)

You're born big as a small bag of sugar
and into your blinkered eyes
and assisted breathing we all whisper grow, grow.
Your uncle says that Max is the best name for a baby fighter
and you do grow and you do fight.
Into the draining of your lungs
the surgeons hum their own mantras.
When Lola visits your heart rate rises.
Her voice holds you, brings you strength
from fisher families stretching right back.
You start to smile and the nurse called Pearl
says you are the best kind of baby
because you are Polish-German-Filipino-Italian-Anglo-Celt.
He'll only ever go to war with himself.
But you don't and you keep growing
and you are peaceable
even when we lug both you and the oxygen around.
We take you to see the Royal de Luxe puppets
stomping about town
and a friend dubs you tiny giant
which you are in my mind
from that day forward.
On a rainy day
you say *Pet City* is as good as the zoo
as if you had a tender heart for small scale ventures.
I wean you on to sweetened tea,
baby-fighter,
and together we take the spoon and stir.

Waiting for Jonathan

On the day of the night you are born,
outside my window
the kestrel keeps patiently tending
her quiet nest
and the tele-tower spins around:
it's *Good Morning London* yet again,
an exclamation point
flashing into the monochromes
of leafless boughs and disowned wintry decks.

Restless the night before,
and thinking of your mother labouring,
I start a family tree,
watching at first in delight
its spectral auto-populations
all heading south to one small parish,
a reprise of names and occupations
as if my ancestors came out of a DIY kit;
then becoming enraged at the Mormon search engine:
no extra-marital partners and lines snuffing out,
petering out with many of the women,
when why should that be so?
And feeling lost, unmoored, wild,
I thought, but not today little one, not today.
Across the pond you are making yourself known.

Into that day and still no news.
In my mother's hand-me-down handbag
a note of hers I kept headed
'My Whereabouts'.
In my jetlag, sharing her initials,
I wonder is it me whose location is in doubt.
But it is your whereabouts, dear heart,
at this pressing moment, at this precise moment,
of which I can't be sure of yet, of which I can't let go.

I catch a clipper
and land outside The Globe
where the Transport for London sign
cheerily proclaims in another exclamation
Thou art here.
Thank Christ and all the Apostles
is all I can muster in reply.
We are found.
I wander aimlessly by the Thames
and her miraculous traffic...
Thou art here thou art here Isis laps...
A seagull flaps into my phone's distracted lens
so flukily, so lively-like
and tethers my heart back to my nest-
building kestrel across the town.
I have watched her at daybreak and nightfall
as bells rang out from a church I never bothered to find.
Your family tree
so much your own
will be what you make it.

Track or lose it, never mind,
we run on, carry on.

Very early the next day,
your father's voice joyous and uncertain
is netted into my bedsit
by the faithful tower.
O good morning! Yes, good morning!
Tomorrow my eyes will fall not here
but on the city of your birth and snow!

Night List

I sleep with a cat and a man.
I sleep with the man every night.
The cat I share with a neighbour.
I sleep beneath the Navajo patterned knee rug
the daughter left behind,
and also, when it is cold, her brown cardigan.
I sleep in socks a little too large,
blue, marl, again left behind, this time by the son
who told me the other day he had found peace.
I am building this armour in my bed
of the man, the cat, the rug, the socks.
It wards off how I begin to feel when the air gets dark.
Beneath the armour is my body, of course,
which has not always been the most reliable of bodies.
But I begin to invent a companion anatomy of goods
that abide in its dark cavity,
eggs hiding maybe even now?
Are they, I read somewhere,
eggs that were in your grandmothers and right back beyond?
And also another thing I read,
in it are housed remnants of the children I have had:
boy, boy, girl – I do hope that is so –
my own boy, boy, girl, man, cat,
rug, cardigan, socks, eggs, remnants
of those carried and born.
Rain outside now making its own patient list.
We're all accounted for here and good.

Little Ditty

At the supermarket
I fail to civilise myself.
I skitter about,
an unruly top,
rolling to the nether ends –
the raw end –
the blood & bone end.
Try as I might
I cannot gain
the centre aisles,
the goods in cans, packets, boxes.

I am an irregularity
in a space of ironed-out irregularities.
Or if these are entirely impossible to eradicate
they are bagged up
and made a virtue of at the raw end.

I've grown old
with the soundtrack in here,
with my hapless compadres
bloody Jack & Diane
who are apparently, like me,
still doing the best they can.

Acknowledgements

Thanks to the editors of the following anthologies and journals in which some of these poems first appeared: *Australian Book Review*, *Australian Poetry Journal*, *Axon*, *Best Australian Poems 2017*, *The Canberra Times*, *Causeway/Cabhair*, *Cordite*, *Contemporary Australian Feminist Poetry: The Hunter Anthology*, *Griffith Review*, *Island*, *Kenyon Review*, *Meanjin*, *Portside Review*, *Prayers for a Secular World*, *Southerly*, *Stilts*, *Strange Cargo: Five Australian Poets*, *Verity La*, and *Writ Review*.

Warm thanks to Ivor Indyk and Aleesha Paz at Giramondo, and also to my family and friends for their encouragement – especially to Tim Dolin.

I acknowledge the continuing culture of the Whadjuk Noongar people, the traditional custodians of the land on which I work and live.

This project has been assisted by the Australian Government through the Australia Council, its arts funding and advisory body.

References

John Berger epigraph. *Confabulations* (London: Penguin Books, 2016), p. 29.

Don DeLillo epigraph. *Zero K* (Sydney: Pan Macmillan, 2016), p. 227.

Epigraph to 'Sudbury's Wilds': Thomas Gainsborough to Thomas Harvey 22 May 1788. In John Hayes (ed.), *The Letters of Thomas Gainsborough* (New Haven: Yale University Press, 2001), no. 108.

Deborah Levy epigraph. *The Man Who Saw Everything* (London: Hamish Hamilton, 2019), p. 77.

Paul Nash epigraph. 'Monster Field' (1939). In Andrew Causey (ed.), *Paul Nash: Writings on Art* (Oxford: Oxford University Press, 2000), p. 150.

Epigraph to 'Girl on a Rug with a Cat': Gillian Wearing. 'Everything is Connected in Life...' 1992–3, Tate, London.

A Lakeland Wardrobe owes a debt to Adam Nicolson's *The Making of Poetry: Coleridge, the Wordsworths and Their Year of Marvels* (William Collins: London, 2019).

About the author

Lucy Dougan's first poetry book, *Memory Shell,* won the Mary Gilmore Award. The manuscript of her second collection, *White Clay,* won the Arts ACT Alec Bolton Award – it was published by Giramondo in 2008. Her chapbooks *Meanderthals* (Web Del Sol) and *Against Lawns* (Picaro) were published in 2011. Her third collection, *The Guardians* (Giramondo, 2015), was shortlisted for both the Judith Wright Calanthe Award and the Victorian Premier's Literary Award for Poetry, and won the 2016 West Australian Premier's Poetry Award. She works in the arts and university sectors.